Flavours of Andaman

A Fusion of Flavors from Land and Sea

Chef ASHWAR PAL SINGH

BlueRose ONE.com
Stories Matter
NewDelhi • London

BLUEROSE PUBLISHERS
India | U.K.

BlueRose ONE.com
Stories Matter
NewDelhi • London

For permissions requests or inquiries regarding this publication,
please contact:

BLUEROSE PUBLISHERS
www.BlueRoseONE.com
info@bluerosepublishers.com
+91 8882 898 898
+4407342408967

ISBN: 978-93-6261-341-7

Cover design: Suruchi
Typesetting: Rohit

First Edition: May 2024

Flavours of Andaman

Far from all the pollution, rush & speed a chain of 572 islands, it's beautiful living in the womd of the Bay of Bengal.

The green canopy and the blue sea just make the perfect combination and we have named them Andaman and Nicobar Islands. The diagnosis is so high that on the one hand Asia's beautiful beach Radha Nagar and we have India's only active volcano 'Banner islands ' our heritage is pride and cellular Jail still speech out the freedom fight. Netaji Subhas Chandra island is just not a tourist spot but it has a huge history that says how fearlessly Netaji hosted our first Indian flag and announced freedom on our island.

Our heritage is incomplete with our tribes, Andaman & Nicobar have 6 different species of tribes which some of are still isolated from the world.

Our island is not only rich in its heritage, and geogricoly wonder but it is also known as mini India.

Andaman & Nicobar Island is one of the beautiful parts of India which is the biggest example of diversity. People from different parts of India have migrated here and from different comer, people have bought different cultures and foods.

Andaman & Nicobar Island are full of different people, cultures, languages, life style & food. Food is the culture here, you will get the best chole bhature, idli sambar, biryani and pethas in one land.

Andaman is a land of flavours which come from home kitchens, restaurants & steels. Exploring see can amaze tourists and some go with the seafood, a huge option of seafood is making Andaman a tourist hub.

Andaman & Nicobar is known for its diversity, which exactly means our Island has a variety in language culture, food & spices. Spices are one of the best gems of our Island, every year we cultivate huge amounts of coconut, black pepper, cloves, cinnamon, nutmeg & many more spices.

Cultivation doesn't stop with spices but we grow a variety of rice, pulses, and vegetables too. Andaman is rich with fauna and a variety of seafoods and it is a blessing, here we have XL-size crabs, lobsters, prawns, and different types of fish.

Andaman is a hub for foodies. The food on our Island is our legacy and with every modern touch, it is getting better.

This book will surely make many people break the old mindset of Kalapani and will help them to include in the new flavours of Andaman.

Contents

Hara Bhara Grill Fish........ 31

A great blend of green masala, mint leaves, coconut, coriander leaves, green chillies, ginger, garlic, onion, and mustard, marinated with fish and grilled pan-fried with butter & charcoal to enhance the flavour and showcase the breeze of our island

Fish steam in Banana Leaves........ 35

Fish with ground ingredients, coconut, mustard seeds, chillies, coriander leaves, mint leaves, salt & mustard oil when marinated to fish & steamed in banana leaves bring and show the culture of our heritage

Prawns Coconut Masala........ 39

The most amazing taste of the seafood, the prawns when cooked with coconut, red chillies, haldi, dhaniya, jeera, green chillies, mustard oil, ginger garlic cooked together, it is present the culture in your plate

Crispy Prawn's Salt and Pepper........ 45

Prawns marinate with flours & spices and deep fried in a hot oil, and usage of some onion & capsicum to toss with salt & pepper with create the magic in our plate

Crab Creamy Rassa........ 49

When crab is cooked, it's aroma speaks everything and is combined with coconut milk, spices, chilli paste and coriander leaves to cook together to showcase our island cuisine

Lobster Delight........ 53

The most popular lobster of our island when fried and cooked with sauce and pepper & chilly flakes with butter, gives the recipe a unique & most selling dish of our paradise

Desi Chicken Curry........ 57

A desi chicken, full of flavour when cooked with whole spices & powder masala in mustard oil with coconut milk gives richness and simple cooking but the best flavour of the desi murgi of our island

Chicken Coconut Curry with Malhabari Paratha........ 61

Coconut grind with chillies, curry leaves, cardamom, long, cinnamon, whole coriander, and jeera and when fried together with chicken and ghee & mustard brings the taste of authenticity and when it is eaten with the Malabari paratha will show the culture of our island

Ghee Roasted Chicken........ 67

A great combination of ghee & chicken with some unique whole spices & ground masalas with red chillies & coriander give the dish a very rich flavour and a modern touch to the recipe

Flavours of Andaman

A Fusion of Flavors from Land and Sea

Chef
ASHWAR PAL SINGH

Nature Ki Bhindi

Ingredients

1. Bhindi
2. Refined Oil
3. Ginger
4. Onion
5. Mustard Oil
6. Green Chilies
7. Bay Leaf
8. Red Chilli Powder
9. Haldi Powder
10. Dhaniya Powder
11. Jeera Powder
12. Garam Masala
13. Coconut Milk
14. Dhaniya patti
15. Curry Leaves
16. Salt to Taste

Methods

- Take a pan or a kadhai and put half a ltr of refined oil and put it on a medium flame and make it hot.
- Take Bhindi according to the quantity you need (we are making for 4 people) half kg, cut it into finger size and out on a side.
- When the oil is heated put your Bhindi in hot oil and deep fry it when the Bhindi comes half-cooked, take it out on a plate.
- Take a kadhai or a pan put 4 tablespoons of refined oil and let it hot, put mustard seed and curry leaves let it cracker for 30 seconds, put bay leaf and sliced onion and steer it for one minute let it become nice and golden pink.
- when the onion becomes pink add ginger garlic paste of tablespoon and steer it for 30 seconds, when the ginger garlic paste is cooked put dry masalas, half a teaspoon of chilli powder, half a teaspoon of haldi powder, one teaspoon of Dhaniya powder, half teaspoon of Jeera powder and out some water to let the masala cooked together for one minute on a low heat.
- When the masala is cooked low flame the gas and add a two diamond cut onion into the pan and cook it for one minute, when the onion becomes soft add one glass of thick coconut milk and simmer it for two minutes on a low flame.
- When the milk comes to a boil add your deep-fried Bhindies and a slice of green chillies and let it cook for another two minutes together on medium-low heat.
- Add chopped coriander leaves and $1/4^{th}$ teaspoon of garam masala to make the dish balanced and add salt according to your taste.
- Enjoy the recipe and try it in your kitchen because recipe says I am the flavour of Andaman.

Cashewnut Caulflower Curry

Ingredients

1. Cashew nut
2. Cauliflower
3. Onion
4. Green chilies
5. Red chilies
6. Ghee
7. Refined oil
8. Ginger garlic paste
9. Haldi powder
10. Chili powder
11. Jeera powder
12. Milk
13. Salt to taste
14. Cashewnut paste
15. Garam masala
16. Coriander leaves
17. Tomato paste

Methods

- Take a bowl and cut pieces of cauliflower and marinate it with some salt and 1 teaspoon of haldi powder and salt to taste keep on a side. Meanwhile, take a kadhai and put 3-4 cups of oil and heat on a high flame when the oil gets hot deep fry the marinated cauliflower one by one and once it is done keep on a side.
- Take a kadhai and put 2 tablespoon of ghee along with 3-4 tablespoons of oil and heat it once the ghee and oil get heated up add one cup of onion paste and chopped green chilies and fry it well for 10 minutes on a medium-low flame. Once the onion is cooked add 2 tablespoons of ginger garlic paste and 1 tomato paste and a half cup of water to allow the masala to cook on a medium low f lame for 5-7 minutes.
- Once the masala cooked and leaves the oil add one teaspoon of haldi powder, 1 tablespoon of chili powder, 1teaspoon of dhaniya powder, and 1 teaspoon of jeera powder and mix well and put a few drops of water to help the masala to cook properly.
- Once the masala is cooked add the soaked and fresh cashew nutscashew nuts and mix well for 5 minutes. After 5 minutes add 2 cups of milk and 2 tablespoons of cashewnut paste to make the curry rich and tasty and cook for 10 minutes on a low flame, after 10 minutes when the curry change its color and the oil is separated, add half cup of water to settle the curry and allow it to comes into a boil.
- When it started boiling add your fried cauliflower to the gravy and allow it to cook for another 5 minutes on a low flame after 5 minutes turn off the gas and put 1 teaspoon of garam masala and some chopped coriander leaves to complete the recipe
- The recipe is rich and full of flavors with the richness of cashew nutand cauliflower and the spices used in the recipe.

- You can serve the recipe along with parathas or rice to create the magic moment for your family and bring happiness with " Flavors of Andaman"

Kathal Ki Biryani

Ingredients

1. Kathal (Jackfruit)
2. Ginger
3. Garlic
4. Red chilli Powder
5. Haldi Powder
6. Jeera Powder
7. Garam masala
8. Curd
9. Mustard oil
10. Refined oil
11. Onion
12. Tomatoes
13. Green chillies
14. Dhaniya patta
15. Mint leaves
16. Good quality Basmati rice
17. Dalchini
18. Bay leaves
19. Javitri
20. Salt to taste
21. Lemon juice
22. Milk
23. Sugar
24. Ghee
25. Red food colour

Methods

- Take a kathal clean it nicely and cut it into cubes according to you, wash the kathal cubes and wash it in water and drain the excess water.
- Let's marinate the kathal with red chilli powder, Haldi powder, Jeera powder, half a teaspoon of Garam masala, two teaspoons of ginger garlic paste, 4 tablespoons of curd, 3 tablespoons, mustard oil, chopped green chillies according to your taste and mix well all together and keep on rest for half an hour.
- Mean while take half a kg of good quality basmati rice wash for 3 to 4 times a nd let it soak in water for half an hour to 45 minutes.
- Take a kadhai or a pan put half a ltr of refined oil and let it heat for ten minutes on medium heat when the oil becomes hot deep fry two big slices of onion and deep fry it on a golden brown called birista.
- On the same hot oil deep fry your marinated kathal to a half cooked way take it out from the oil and keep it on a side.
- Now the time to make the masala take a pan or a kadhai put two tablespoons of oil and two tablespoons of ghee and let it heat for one minute on a medium-low flame when the oil turns hot put your whole spices like dalchini, bay leaves, javitri, slice onion, green chilli together and until it becomes soft.
- Now add two tablespoons ginger garlic paste to an onion and let it cook together for one minute now add deep fried kathals on a pan and mix well with the onion and ginger garlic paste and cook it for two minutes on a high flame.
- Now it the tim e to add your dry spices one teaspoon of chilli powder, one teaspoon of jeera powder, one teaspoon of dhaniya

powder, and chopped tomatoes and mix well add 1/4th glass of water to help the masalas and kathal to cook together for 5 minutes on a low flame close the lid.

- When the masala is cooked add 4-5 tablespoons of beaten curd on a low flame and mix well and cook it for 5 minutes, after 5 minutes when it releases the water add garam masala, coriander leaves, and sliced green chillies, turn off the gas put the lid on and keep it on a side.
- This is the time to make your rice take 1 Ltr of water on a vessel and turn on the heat on a full flame, into the water add 3 tablespoons of salt, into two pieces of dalchini, two pieces of javitri , 4 bay leaves, 4 tablespoons of refined oil and let it come into a boil.
- When the water is boiling add your soaked rice and cook it for 10 minutes on a high flame. cook the rice when it is half done reduce the flame to low and time to layer your Biryani.
- Take a pan or a heavy vessel, put one tablespoon of ghee on the base, put half of the rice in the bottom of the pan, add fried onions on the surface of the rice pinch of garam masala, mint leaves 2 to 3 tablespoons of milk, half teaspoon of liquid red food color and the in the first layer is done.
- Let's add the second layer of your kathal masala into the pan how make the 3rd layer of the remaining rice into the pan and add fried onion, mint leaves a pinch of garam masala, half a teaspoon of red food color, 2 to 3 spoons of milk to give the flavour in our biryani.
- Put the remaining kathal masala as a fourth layer in our biryani and add the fried onion and mint leaves to complete the process sealed the pot or the vessel with aluminum foil or a doe of wheat flour to seal the pot according to your choice.
- Keep the pot on a low flame for 10 minutes into dum, after 10 to 15 minutes turn off the flame and let it cool for another 10-15 minutes now open the vessel of a pan and feel the magic in the air for the flavours coming out from the pot and says the flavors of Andaman.
  (Enjoy)

Drumstick and Pumpkin Coconut Curry

Ingredients

1. Pumpkin
2. Drumsticks
3. Coconut milk
4. Mustard oil
5. Curry leaves
6. Mustard seeds
7. Whole dhaniya
8. Whole jeera
9. Whole red chilli
10. Haldi powder
11. Salt to taste
12. Green chillies
13. Ginger
14. Garlic
15. Black pepper
16. Whole saunf

Methods

- Peel the drumsticks and cut them out of your choice. Take a pumpkin and cut it into a small cub both washed properly and keep it on a side now the time to roast our whole spices.
- Take a pan put one tablespoon a saunf, whole dhaniya, whole jeera, 5-6 whole red chillies, and half a teaspoon of black pepper corn and roast it for 5-7 minutes on a medium-low heat. When it cools down grind the spices and keep them on the side.
- Take a kadhai or a pan put 4 tablespoons of mustard oil and let it heat on a medium-low flame for 5-7 minutes, when the oil becomes hot add half a teaspoon of mustard seeds and curry leaves and let it crackers for 30 seconds add one slice onion and cook it until it becomes soft.
- Add 1 teaspoon of chopped teaspoon of garlic and mix well with the onion for 30 seconds. Now is the time to add your pumpkin and drumsticks to the kadhai or a pan mix well together and let it cook for 10-12 minutes on a low flame.
- After 10 minutes when it becomes softer add your ground masalas 2 tablespoons, salt to taste, and half a teaspoon of haldi powder and steer it well to give a good mix together and add have a glass of water and cook it for 5 minutes on a medium-low flame.
- After 5 minutes low the heat and add coconut milk 1 ½ glass according to the curry you need and mix well and cook it for 10 minutes on a low flame.
- Now the time turn off the heat and add coriander leaves and green chilies to balance the dish and serve to your loved ones and say.
- "flavour of Andaman"
- You can enjoy the dish with parathas or steam rice.

Gosht Bharva Karela

Ingredients

1. Karela
2. Chicken (Boneless)
3. Saunf
4. Jeera
5. Onion seeds
6. Black pepper
7. Whole red chillies
8. Mustard oil
9. Onions
10. Green chillies
11. Dhaniya patti
12. Curry leaves
13. Salt to taste
14. Coconut

Methods

- Take half a kg of karelas peel it nicely apply salt and rub in the karela keep it on the side for one hour.
- Now the time to roast our dry masalas 2 teaspoons of Saunf, 1 teaspoon of jeera, 1 teaspoon of kala jeera, ½ teaspoon of black pepper, and 4 whole red chilies, roast it all together on a low flame for 5-7 minutes and take it out and cool down.
- In the same pan ad d 2 tablespoons of coconut and dry roast until it becomes golden and take it out on the same dry roast masala together, when the spices and coconut cool down grind it together and make a powder.
- Now chop 2 onions, 3-4 green chilies some coriander leaves and take them out on a bowl, In the same bowl add your ground masalas along with 3-4 tablespoons of mustard oil and salt to taste and mix well take a boneless chicken and cut it into small cubes and mix with the onion mixture.
- Take a kadhai and put 7-8 tablespoons of mustard oil on a medium-low flame and until it becomes hot.
- Meanwhile wash your karelas in water drain out the excess water and rub it with the cloth until the karelas become dry.
- Now the time to put the chicken mixture inside the karelas one by one after you finish refill the chicken mixture into the karelas time to seal it one by one take a thread and seal it one by one by rotating the threads to seal it.
- Now the time to fry the karelas on a low flame for half an hour after half an hour when the karelas become soft and the chicken cooked time to add 2 tablespoons of tamarind pulp and cook it for another 10 minutes on a low flame.
- Switch off the gas and serve it with Parathas or rice to feel the flavors and say.

  "flavors of Andaman"

Coconut Fish Curry

Ingredients

1. Fish (as per your choice)
2. Mustard oil
3. Ginger garlic paste
4. Haldi powder
5. Red chilli powder
6. Mix masala
7. Salt to taste
8. Coriander leaves
9. Curry leaves
10. Mustard seeds
11. Tamarind pulp
12. Coconut milk
13. Onion

Methods

- To marinate the fish, fish of your choice take a bowl, add one tablespoon of ginger garlic paste, one tablespoon of haldi powder, one tablespoon of chilli powder, one tablespoon of mustard oil, salt according to your taste and mix well and add your fish on the marination and mix everything and keep it on a side for 10 minutes.
- Take a pan or a kadhai heat it for a few seconds and put 3-4 tablespoons of mustard oil and keep flame high. When the oil gets hot add one teaspoon of mustard seeds and Curry leaves on a hot oil to crackle. Add one cup of sliced onion and mix well.
- When the onion turns to soft add one tablespoon of ginger garlic paste and let, the paste cook until the smell goes out. After that add one teaspoon of haldi powder, one teaspoon of chilli powder, one teaspoon of mixed masala and put some water, and cook for 30-40 seconds on a high flame.
- When the oil gets separated from the masala, add your marinated fish mix with the masala close the pan with the lid, and keep the gas on a low flame for 10 minutes.
- When the fish is cooked properly with the masala, now the time to add one big glass of coconut milk and add salt according to your taste, and let it cook for another 5 minutes on a low flame.
- After 5 minutes when it comes to a boil add coriander leaves and serve the coconut fish curry with some hot steamed rice to your family and friends to enjoy the moment and say.

  "flavours of Andaman"

Hara Bhara Grill Fish

Ingredients

1. Whole fish (according to the size)
2. Ginger garlic paste
3. Lemon juice
4. Coriander leaves
5. Green chilies
6. Pepper powder
7. Red chilli powder
8. Salt to taste
9. Mustard oil
10. Butter
11. Mint leaves
12. Cumin powder

Methods

- Take a fish, wash and clean it properly with the help of a kitchen towel or tissue paper, and dry the fish.
- Once you dry the fish take a knife and have a 4-5 cut marks at the center of the fish to give it a slit. After you finish the cut marks now it's time to make a marination. For that, you need to make a paste. Take a mixer jar and add one cup of coriander leaves, 1 cup of mint leaves, squeeze 1 whole lemon, salt to taste, add a teaspoon of chilichili powder, ½ teaspoon of cumin powder, a quarter teaspoon of pepper powder, and 2 tablespoons of mustard oil, 2 green chilies and grind it well to make a smooth paste.
- Apply the paste and marinate the fish inside and outside of the fish into the slit part and leave it for half an hour to get marinated well. After half an hour add 1 teaspoon of ginger garlic paste and salt to taste and leave it for another 15 minutes.
- Once it's marinated well and the fish absorbs the masala, now it's time to grill the fish. Take a grilled pan and apply some butter on a medium-low flame and a few drops of mustard oil once the pan gets hot put your marinated fish and grill toss both sides for 5-7 minutes each sides. After grilling from both sides, apply some butter on top and grill again to give a charcoal texture.
- Once the fish is ready from both sides serve it hot with green chutney, lemon, and onion to give a compliment to the dish and serve it hot to your family and friends to enjoy the "flavorus of Andaman"

Fish steam in banana leaves

Ingredients

1. Fish (on your choice)
2. Green chilies
3. Ginger garlic paste
4. Coconut
5. Haldi powder
6. Mustard oil
7. Chilli powder
8. Salt to taste
9. Curry leaves
10. Coriander leaves
11. Mustard seeds
12. Banana leaves
13. Lemon juice

Methods

- Take a whole fish or a cut piece according to the size, marinate it with some salt, turmeric, and lemon juice, and keep aside for 10 minutes.
- Time to make paste take a mixing jar and put coconut, some mustard seeds, 1 teaspoon of ginger garlic paste, 15-16 pieces of curry leaves 4 green chillies, 1 tablespoon of mustard seeds, salt according to your taste, and grind well to make a smooth paste.
- Take a piece of banana leaves and roast the banana leaves on a pan or tawa to make it softer.
- When the banana leaves are roasted well now is the time to place the smooth paste 1-2 spoon paste on the surface of the banana leaves and spread it out on the center. When the first layer is done place the marinated fish one by one in different banana leaves apply the smooth paste on the top surface of the fish and cover the fish with the smooth paste.
- When the fish is fully covered with a smooth paste, now the time to make parcels gently fold the sides to make a packet, and with the help of a rope seal the leaf gently.
- Time to steam the fish you can apply on a steamer or a pan to steam the fish for 15-20 minutes and after 20 minutes switch off the flame and leave it for another 5 -7 minutes in its heat.
- Now the time to plate the cooked banana leaves fish on a plate and serve with rice or chapattis to your family and friends to enjoy the "flavours of Andaman"

Prawns Coconut Masala

Ingredients

1. Prawns
2. Whole Dhaniya
3. Whole jeera
4. Whole peppercorns
5. Red chilies
6. Onion
7. Green chilli
8. Curry leaves
9. Ginger garlic paste
10. Haldi powder
11. Mix masala
12. Chilli powder
13. Mustard oil
14. Salt to taste
15. Coriander leaves
16. Coconut
17. Lemon
18. Bay leaf
19. Cinnamon
20. Coconut milk

Methods

- Firstly we will marinate the prawns, for take a bowl and put your washed and clean prawns along with 1 tablespoon of ginger garlic paste ½ a lemon juice quarter teaspoon of haldi powder, and a pinch of salt and marinate well and keep aside.
- Now the time is to roast the dry ingredients 1 teaspoon of peppercorn, 1 tablespoon of dhaniya seeds, 1 teaspoon of jeera seeds and 5-6 whole red chilies dry roast the whole spices on a low flame, for 5-7 minutes when the spices roasted well and you will feel the aromas from the pan, this is the time to add your peel coconut 1 cup and dry roast until it changes its colour into golden. When the coconut get roasted properly take out from the pan and keep it on a plate for 5 minutes until it comes to room temperature.
- Now, once the coconut comes to room temperature grind the coconut into a smooth powder or paste with the help of water.
- Now is the time to make our prawns on a pan. Take a pan or a kadhai and heat up into a low medium-low flame. Once the pan gets hot add half a cup of mustard oil and allow it to get burn on a high flame. When the oil is hot add 1 cup of sliced onion, 3-4 bay leaves, 1 piece of cinnamoncinnamon stick, a few curry leaves and mix well and cook for few minutes until it turns the color into pink.
- When the onion turns the color into pink add 2-3 red chilies and 1 tablespoon of ginger garlic paste mix well and allow it to cook until the smell goes out of ginger garlic from the pan.
- Once the ginger garlic is cooked and the oil gets separated from the pan, lower the flame and add your dry ingredients. A quarter teaspoon of haldi powder, ½ teaspoon of chilli powder, half teaspoon of mix masala and mix well with the help of a few drops

of water to allow the masala to cook. After few minutes when the masala gets cooked and the oil gets separated add your marinated prawns into the masala and cook well for 5 minutes on a high flame and add salt to taste.

- After 5 minutes low flame the gas add 2 tablespoons of your coconut grind masala into the prawns and cook for another 3-4 minutes on a low flame. Add half a cup of thick coconut milk and cook for another 5 minutes on medium-low heat and once the prawns release the oil time to turn off the gas and sever on a bowl, garnish with some coriander leave and chopped red chilies on top and sever hot with some chapattis or rice to your family and friends to bring the best memories of "flavor of Andaman"

Crispy prawn's salt and pepper

Ingredients

1. Prawns
2. Ginger garlic paste
3. Pepper powder
4. Salt to taste
5. Lemon juice
6. Rice flour
7. Corn flour
8. Bread crumbs
9. Egg
10. Refined oil

Methods

- Take a bowl and marinate the prawns with 1 teaspoon of ginger garlic paste, 1 teaspoon of black pepper, salt to taste, and 2 whole lemons juice and mix well and leave it for 10-15 minutes.
- After 15 minutes add one whole beaten egg and mix with the prawns and leave it for 5 more minutes.
- Take a bowl and make a slurry of 4 tablespoons of rice flour, 2 tablespoons of corn flour a quarter cup of water and mix well and make a thick slurry add salt and pepper it, and leave it for 5 minutes.
- Take a pan or a kadhai put half a ltr of refined oil and heat it on a full flame.
- Take your bread crumbs on a plate keep them on a side and make your prawns ready for deep fry, for the process take your prawns one by one deep on the slurry, and coat them with the bread crumbs and make them ready on a plate for deep fry.
- When the oil gets hot leave the prawns one by one into the hot oil and deep fry it for 5-6 minutes and do the remaining process one by one.
- When all the prawns get fried now sprinkle some salt and pepper from the top along with some dip hot chutney for your family and friends to enjoy the moment and say.

  "flavour of Andaman "

Crab Creamy Rassa

Ingredients

1. Crab ½ kg
2. Coconut milk
3. Fresh cream
4. Green chillies
5. Black pepper
6. Garlic paste
7. Onion paste
8. Salt to taste
9. Coriander leaves
10. Red chilli powder
11. Oil

Methods

- Take a pan put 3 tablespoons of oil pan and heat it, put onion paste and fry it for 5 to 6 minutes on a low flame
- Add one tablespoon of garlic paste into the onion paste mix well and fry for another 5 minutes on a low flame
- Add crap into the pan and mix well on a high flame for 5-6 minutes now add salt to taste, red chilli powder ½ teaspoon black pepper, ½ teaspoon, and mix well
- Add ½ ltr fresh coconut milk mix well and boil it for 10 minutes on a medium flame and cover the lid.
- After 10 minutes add 4-5 tablespoons of fresh cream and green chilli 3-4 slices and boil it for 3-4 minutes on a medium flame.
- After 3-4 minutes turn off the gas and take out your Rassa and on a servi ng bowl and garnish with coriander leaves.
- Your crab-creamy Rassa is ready to eat. Serve it with steamed rice or chapatti and enjoy the "flavour of Andaman"

Lobster Delight

Ingredients

1. Lobsters (according to your size)
2. Lemon juice
3. Black pepper powder
4. Salt to taste
5. Refined oil
6. Butter
7. Chilli powder
8. Cream
9. Green chilies
10. Garlic
11. Coriander leaves
12. Chilli flakes

Methods

- Take a lobster and wash it properly from the center make a cut and take out the flush from the lobster clean and wash the lobster again now boil the lobster shells for 10-15 minutes. On a medium-low heat, once the lobster shells change color to red take out from the hot water and keep aside for garnishing.
- Take a bowl and put the lobster's flush cut pieces for the marination process. For marination, put salt to taste, a quarter teaspoon of black pepper powder. One whole lemon juice and 1 tablespoon of refined oil and mix well and keep it aside for 10 minutes.
- After 10 minutes take a pan or kadhai and add 1 tablespoon of butter and 1 tablespoon of oil, the butter and oil gets hot put chopped green chillies half teaspoon and one tablespoon of chopped garlic, fry for 20–25 seconds on a high heat, once the chilies and garlic turns the colour add your marinated lobster into the pan and mix well. Let it get cooked for 1 minute on a high flame.
- After 1 minute low the flame and add one cup of beat powder en-cream, salt according to the taste ,teaspoon of chilli flakes, half teaspoon of black pepper, and cook it for another 2 minutes on a medium-low heat. To make sure that the cream should not be curdle fry it for 2-3 minutes more.
- When the crab turns color and the texture becomes thick add 1 tablespoon of chopped fresh coriander leaves to finish the dish and cook for another 1 minute on a medium-low heat.
- Now the time to plate the cooked lobster into the boiled lobster shells with some rice or chapatis to serve to your family and friends to embrace the "flavours of Andaman "

Desi Chicken Curry

Ingredients

1. Desi chicken
2. Mustard oil
3. Green chilli
4. Ginger garlic paste
5. Haldi powder
6. Chilli powder
7. Mix masala
8. Garam masala
9. Curry leaves
10. Onion
11. Bay leaf
12. Tomatoes

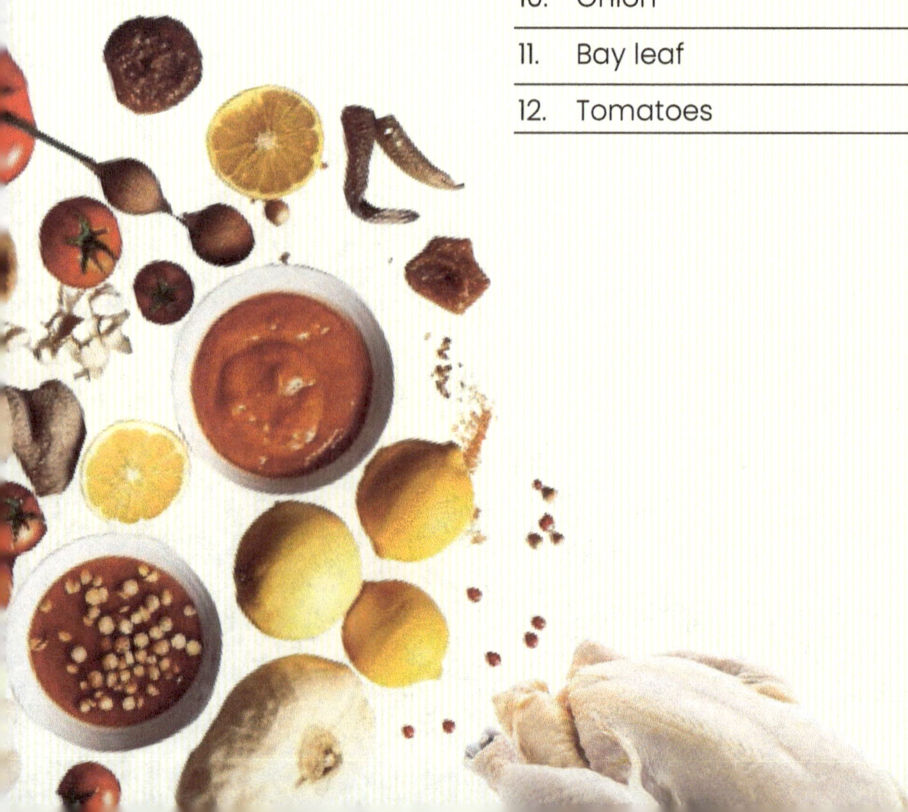

Methods

- Take a pressure cooker and heat it up. When the cooker gets hot put one cup of mustard oil and heat on a high flame once the heat gets hot add bay leaf, green chilies, and 3-4 sliced onions, and cook well until the onion changes color to pink.
- When the onion changes its colour add 3 tablespoons of ginger garlic paste and fry it well until the smell of ginger garlic goes out when it is fried well add 1 teaspoon of haldi powder, 2 teaspoons chilli powder,3 tablespoons of mix masala, 2 chopped tomatoes and mix well and apply half glass of water to help the masala to cook.
- When the oil gets separated from the masala add the desi chicken and fry it well until the juices come out from the chicken.
- When the juices are coming out from the chicken add one glass of water and salt to taste and some chopped coriander, mix everything and pressure cook the chicken for 5-6 whistle.
- After 5-6 whistle turn off gas and let cook for 15 minutes on its own heat.
- After 15 minutes when it cool down and the pressure comes out open the cooker and put 2 teaspoon of garam masala and serve the desi chicken curry along with hot plain rice or chapatis according to your choice to your family and friends to enjoy the "flavours of Andaman"

Chicken Coconut Curry With Malhabari Paratha

Ingredients

1. Chicken
2. Onion
3. Ginger Garlic paste
4. Green chilli
5. Coconut
6. Coconut milk
7. Curry leaves
8. Mustard seeds
9. Coriander leaves
10. Chilli powder
11. Haldi powder
12. Dhaniya powder
13. Garam masala
14. Pepper powder
15. Jeera
16. Tamarind pulp
17. Salt to taste\
18. Mustard oil
19. Tomatoes

(FOR PARATHA)

Maida

Salt

Refined Oil

Water

Methods

CHICKEN COCONUT CURRY

- Take a kadhai or a pan and allow the pan to heat on a medium flame when the pan gets hot put 5-6 tablespoons of mustard oil and allow the oil to get heat on a high flame, once the oil gets hot add 1 cup of sliced onion and 3-4 green chilies along with some curry leaves and steer it well and allow the onion to get soft on medium-low heat to 5 minutes.
- When the onion turns the color into pink add two tablespoons of ginger garlic paste and mix well until the smell goes out of the ginger garlic, after the onion is cooked add freshly chopped tomatoes and cook for another 5 minutes. Once the tomatoes get cooked add 2 tablespoons of dhaniya powder 1 teaspoon of haldi powder and 2 teaspoons of chilli powder and put a half cut of water to allow the masala to cook on a low flame for 5 minutes.
- Once the masala gets cooked add your chicken pieces of 1 kg and mix everything together and allow the chicken and the masala to cook together for 10-15 minutes on a low flame, meanwhile let make the coconut paste ready for the chicken.
- Take 1 cup of coconut into a mixer jar add coriander leaves 1-2 tablespoon, 2 or 3 green chillies, 1 teaspoon of tamarind pulp and grind the coconut into smooth paste. And keep it on aside.
- After 10 minutes when the chicken releases the oil, add to coconut paste and mix well and cook it for 5-7 minutes on medium low heat. After 7 minutes add 1 glass of coconut milk and salt to taste and mix well and allow the curry comes to a boil and cook for 8-10 minutes. On a low medium-low heat.
- After 10 minutes add ½ cup of water boil it for another 5 minutes on full flame and add freshly chopped coriander leaves to finish your dish.

- Once the dish is ready serve it in a bowl keep on aside and make the complimentary dish served with the chicken coconut curry.
- MALHABARI PARATHA
- Take 2 cups of maida along with ½ teaspoon of salt. Add ½ cup of oil and mix everything well with the help of water bring it into a soft dough and keep aside for at least 15-20 minutes.
- When the dough rested for 20 minutes make a small bowl and put some oil on the surface to make dough in the form of chapatti with the help of a roller and try to roll the dough as much as you can extend the dough and make a circle.
- Now, apply oil on the circle of the dough and start flipping both sides one by one and make a straight line after that start rolling again and make a form of a chakri and keep the same one by one and rest for 5-10 minutes.
- After 10 minutes start the dough and make a form of chapattis one by one and make the tawa heat on a high flame ready now put your parathas into the tawa and cook from both sides equally with the help of oil and make it crispy and do the same process to prepare your remaining parathas.
- Once, you have all the parathas ready keep everything step by step and beat the parathas from all the sides to create the laccha of the Malhabari Parathas.
- Now the time to plate both dishes together and bring the magic of "flavour of Andaman"

Ghee Roasted Chicken

Ingredients

1. Chicken pieces (with bone)
2. Ginger garlic paste
3. Ghee
4. Haldi powder
5. Chilli powder
6. Coriander powder
7. Jeera powder
8. Garam masala powder
9. Whole spices
10. Salt to taste
11. Lemon juice
12. Coriander leaves
13. Curry leaves
14. Red whole chilies
15. Green chilies
16. Kashmiri red chilli powder
17. Onion

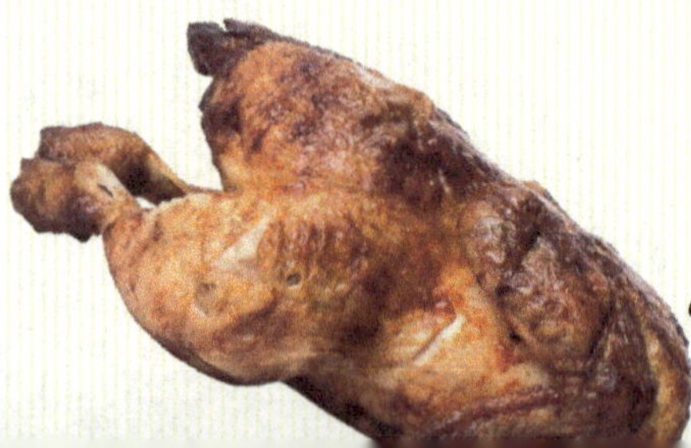

Methods

- To marinate the chicken take bowl and put the cut pieces of chicken in the bowl add 2 tablespoons of ginger garlic paste, 1 teaspoon of haldi powder,1 teaspoon of chilli powder,1 teaspoon of Kashmiri red chilli powder,2 teaspoons of dhaniya powder,1 teaspoon of jeera powder, salt to taste, 2 tablespoon of melted ghee and some curry leaves and marinate well and keep aside and leave for half an hour.
- After half an hour take a pan or kadhai and heat on a medium low flame for 2 minutes, when the pan get hot add 4 tablespoon of ghee and let it heat.
- When the ghee gets hot put whole spices Cardamom, Cinemon, cloves and green chilies and red whole chilies, cook it for 30 seconds. Add 2 whole sliced Onions and fry it well, till the onion changes color into pink.
- When the onion turns the color add 1 tablespoon of ginger garlic paste and fry it well for until the smell goes out of the ginger garlic on a medium low heat. Now add the marinated chicken into the pan mix everything well and fry it for 10-15 minutes on a medium-low flame and cover the pan with the lid.
- After 10 minutes turn the gas into low and roast the chicken for 15 minutes until the chicken reduce the water and comes into a roasted condition and fry it well. After 15 minutes now time to add one teaspoon of garam masala and one teaspoon of chopped coriander leaves mix it well and fry it for another 5 minutes on a low flame.
- After 5 minutes when the chicken is cooked and roasted properly serve it into a plate or a platter and garnish it with sliced ginger and chilies, coriander leaves and lemon according to your choice. Your ghee roasted chicken is ready to sever to your family and friends to enjoy the "flavours of Andaman"

Chicken mahatabi

Ingredients

1. Chicken
2. Onion
3. Ghee
4. Ginger garlic paste
5. Green chilies
6. Dhaniya powder
7. Jeera powder
8. Garam masala
9. Cashew nuts paste
10. Milk
11. Butter
12. Salt to taste
13. Dhaniya patta

Methods

- To make chicken Mahatabi take a kadhai or a pan and turn on heat on medium-low flame, when the pan gets hot put 4 tablespoons of ghee and let it hot.
- When the ghee gets hot add 1 cup of sliced onion, and 7-8 chopped green chilies and let it cook for 5-10 minutes on a medium-low heat once the onion turns colour into golden brown add 1 kg of chicken and steer it well on a full flame.
- After 5-7 minutes add 3-4 teaspoons of ginger garlic paste and mix well and allow the chicken and ginger garlic paste to cook for another 10 minutes on medium low heat. Once the paste gets cooked and chicken turns the colour add 2 tablespoon of dhaniya powder, 1 tablespoon of jeera powder and mix well and put half glass of water to allow the masala to cook chicken combine it well and cook on medium low heat.
- After 5 minutes when the masala is cooked add ½ cup of cashew nut paste and 1 glass of milk to the chicken and mix well and allow the chicken to cook on a low flame for 10 minutes.
- After 10 minutes when the chicken separates the ghee add 1 teaspoon of Garam masala and 1 tablespoon of coriander leaves mix well and cook for another 2 minutes on a low flame.
- After 2 minutes switch off the gas and take out the dish on a bowl or plate and garnish with butter and some coriander leaves to make the chicken Mahatabi ready on the table and serve with some hot chapattis or rice to compliment the dish.
- Your chicken Mahatabi is ready to serve to your family and friends to bring the magic of "flavour of Andaman"

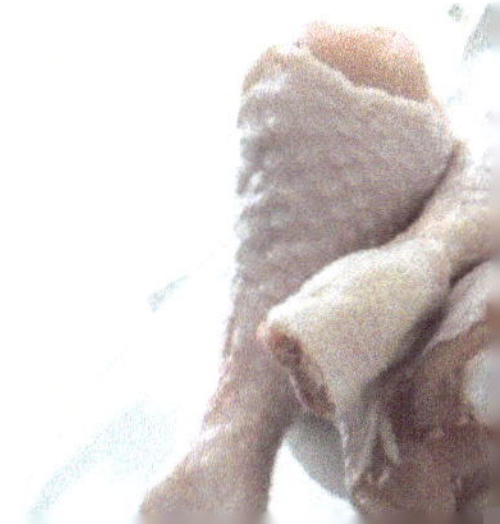

Andamani Mutton Curry

Ingredients

1. Mutton
2. Onion
3. Ginger Garlic Paste
4. Green Chilies
5. Curry Leaves
6. Coriander Leaves
7. Coconut Milk
8. Red Chilies
9. Salt to Taste
10. Mustard Oil
11. Bay Leaf
12. Cinnamon
13. Dhaniya Powder
14. Mix Masala
15. Haldi Powder
16. Chili Powder
17. Jeera Powder
18. Garam Masala
19. Curd

Methods

- Take a heavy pan and make it hot on a high flame when the pan is hot, put 7-8 tablespoonstablespoons of mustard oil and make it hot on a high flame.
- When the oil gets hot add 3-4 bay leaves and 3-4 cinnamon sticks add 2 cups of sliced onion and mix well, after 2 minutes when the onion changes color add your 1 kg of mutton pieces and salt to taste and mix everything well and fry it for 10-15 minutes on a high flame.
- After 15 minutes put 2 glasses of water and allow the mutton to cook for 40 minutes on medium-low heat and close the lid. After 40 minutes open the lid and steer it again and add 1 teaspoon of haldi powder, 2 teaspoons of chili powder, 1 teaspoon of dhaniya powder, 2 tablespoons of mixed masala and 1 teaspoon of jeera powder, and 2 freshly chopped tomatoes and half glass of water to allow the mutton and masala to cook properly on a medium low flame for 10-15 minutes.
- After 15 minutes low the flame add 1 cup of beaten curd and cook the mutton for 15 more minutes until the oil gets separated from the mutton. Once the oil gets separated add 1 glass of coconut milk to enhance the flavor of the curry and cook for another 10 minutes on a low flame.
- After 10 minutes add chopped green chilies and garam masala to finish the dish and mix well. Take a small pan to make a tadka ready to complete the dish. Make a pan hot put 2 tablespoons of ghee and make it hot. When the ghee is hot put 3-4 red chilies and some curry leaves into the ghee and allow it to crackle it. once it crackles put the ghee chilichili and curry leaves into the mutton curry.
- Your Andamani mutton curry is ready to serve along with rice or chapattis or parathas to serve to your family or friend to bring the taste of the "Flavour of Andaman".

Mutton pulav

Ingredients

1. Mutton
2. Basmati rice
3. Elaichi
4. Cinnamon
5. Bay leaves
6. Cloves
7. Onion
8. Tomato
9. Salt to taste
10. Ghee
11. Green chilies
12. Coriander leaves
13. Chilie powder
14. Haldi powder
15. Garam masala
16. Dhaniya powder
17. Water
18. Cashewalnuts
19. Ginger garlic paste
20. Ginger juliens

Methods

- Take a pressure cooker and add 1 kg of mutton pieces along with salt to taste and your whole spices and put one glass of water along with 1 tablespoon of ghee and pressure cook the mutton into 4-5 whistles and turn the gas and keep aside.
- Take 1 kg of basmati rice and soak it into water for ½ hours. Take a pot and heat it on a high flame for 2 minutes, once the pot is hot add bay leaf 2-3 and 1 cup of sliced onion and 5-6 green chilies and fry it well until the onion change colour and turns into golden.
- Till the onion is cooking take out the pressure from the cooker open the lid and take out the mutton pieces one by one into a bowl drain the remaining stalk of the mutton and keep on a side. Once the onion turns thc color add thc mutton and fry it well on a medium-low heat.
- After 5 minutes add 2 tablespoontablespoon of ginger garlic paste and 1 teaspoon of haldi powder and cook well until the smell goes out. After the ginger garlic cooks add 1 tablespoon of dhaniya powder, 1 teaspoon chili powder, 1 teaspoon of garam masala and mix well add 2 chopped tomatoes and mix well. Allow it to cook for another 10 minutes on a low flame.
- Once the masala is cooked add the mutton stock and one cup of hot water to the mutton and allow them to come to a boil. When it's started boiling put the soaked rice into the pot and mix the mutton and rice together and cook for 5 minutes on high flame.
- After 5 minutes pour some rose water and chopped coriander leaves on the top and seal the top with the help of aluminum foil or some cloth and cover it with the lid and allow the pulao to dum for 15-20 minutes on a low flame.
- After 15-20 minutes turn off the gas and allow the pulao to rest for 10 minutes on its heat. After 10 minutes take out the pulao on a

platter or a bowl and garnish with some cashew nut, ginger julien, and coriander leaves to finish the recipe.

- Mutton pulao is one of the recipes that is a single complete meal but you can serve some papad and coriander chutnies and salad to give compliment to the dish and serve to your family and friends to bring the best taste of "Flavors of Andaman"

Nariyal Ki Barfi

Ingredients

1.	Coconuts
2.	Sugar
3.	Milk
4.	Elaichi powder
5.	Food color (Yellow)
6.	Kesar
7.	Pista
8.	Badam
9.	Kaju
10.	Silver/Golden work
11.	Ghee/Oil

Methods

- Take a pan or kadhai, take 1 big bowl of peel coconut, add 1 cup of sugar, and ½ cup of milk, and mix well and keep it on aside for 15-20 minutes and add a pinch of yellow food color.
- After 20 minutes put the pan on gas, on a medium-low flame and fry it for 20 minutes. After 20 minutes once the coconut mixture turns into a form of doe turn off the gas and add ½ teaspoon of elichi powder.
- Take a plate or a barfi setting tray and Greece with some ghee or oil and transfer your coconut mixture into the tray and flatten the mixture to allow the coconut barfi to take shape and set.
- Once you flatten the coconut mixtures apply some silver or gold leaves for garnish and some dry fruits of your choice the top of the barfi. Once you set all the ingredients on top, make sure you should give a cut piece of barfi of your choice or size before it gets set and leave for 1 hour.
- After 1 hour when the barfi sets and becomes hard take out the pieces of the barfi one by one and send them to your family and friends to enjoy the happy moments together and say "flavors of Andaman"

Kaju aur Nariyal ke Laddoos

Ingredients

1. Nariyal (coconut)
2. Broken cashews
3. Jaggery
4. Eliachi powder
5. Coconut milk
6. Dry rose petals
7. Ghee/Oil

Methods

- Take a pan or kadhai add 1 big bowl of peeled coconut, 1 cup of broken cashews, 2 cups up jaggeries, and cup of coconut milk, mix well and keep aside for 10 minutes.
- After 10 minutes turn on the heat keep the pan on the stove and start steering it on a low medium-low flame for 10 minutes. After 10 minutes when the coconut become sticky and the jaggery and milk are reduced. Time to add half a teaspoon of elaichi powder and 2 tablespoon of dry rose petals and fry it for another 5 minutes on a medium low flame.
- After 5 minutes turn the gas off and take out the coconut mixture and spread to cool down. When the mixture comes to a room temperature. Time to make the laddoos according to your size.
- Once you complete the laddoos serve the kaju, Nariyal ke Laddoos to your family and friends and to enjoy the moment of happiness and say it together this is "Flavors of Andaman"

IN LOVING MEMORY OF

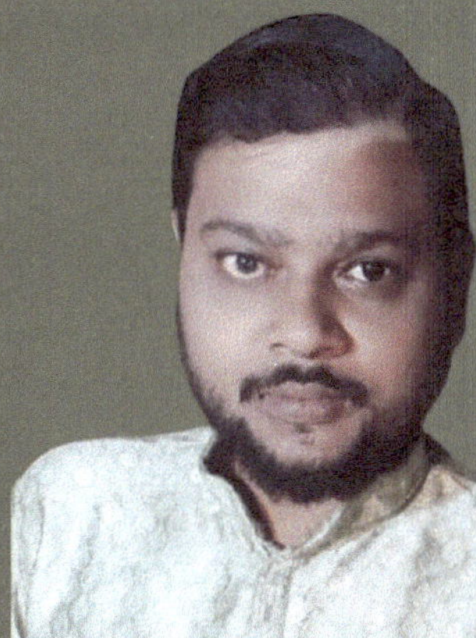

Wasim Akram

IN OUR HEARTS
FOREVER AND ALWAYS...

Your presence brought light to our days, and your laughter will forever echo in our hearts.